Musical Instruments

Trumpet

By Nick Rebman

www.littlebluehousebooks.com

Copyright © 2023 by Little Blue House, Mendota Heights, MN 55120. All rights reserved. No part of this book may be reproduced or utilized in any form or by any means without written permission from the publisher.

Little Blue House is distributed by North Star Editions:
sales@northstareditions.com | 888-417-0195

Produced for Little Blue House by Red Line Editorial.

Photographs ©: Shutterstock Images, cover, 4, 7, 8–9, 11, 13, 14–15, 16–17, 21, 23, 24 (top left), 24 (top right), 24 (bottom left), 24 (bottom right); PNW Production/Pexels, 19

Library of Congress Control Number: 2022910652

ISBN
978-1-64619-702-6 (hardcover)
978-1-64619-734-7 (paperback)
978-1-64619-795-8 (ebook pdf)
978-1-64619-766-8 (hosted ebook)

Printed in the United States of America
Mankato, MN
012023

About the Author

Nick Rebman is a writer and editor who lives in Minnesota. He enjoys reading, walking his dog, and playing rock songs on his drum set.

Table of Contents

Playing My Trumpet **5**

Glossary **24**

Index **24**

Playing My Trumpet

I play my trumpet.

I blow into it.

I play my trumpet.

It makes a sound.

I play my trumpet.

It has three valves.

I play my trumpet.

I press a valve.

It changes the sound.

I play my trumpet.
My teacher helps me get better.

I play my trumpet.

I practice every day.

I play my trumpet.

I read sheet music.

I play my trumpet.

My sister listens to me.

I play my trumpet.

I am in a band.

I play my trumpet.

We play a fun song.

Glossary

band

teacher

sheet music

valves

Index

B
band, 20

P
practice, 14

S
sound, 6, 10

V
valves, 8, 10